CAPITAL ASSET PRICING MODEL

Make smart investment decisions to build a strong portfolio

Written by Ariane de Saeger
In collaboration with Isabelle Van Steenkiste
Translated by Carly Probert

Business 50MINUTES.com

CAPITAL ASSET PRICING MODEL

KEY INFORMATION

- **Names:** Capital asset pricing model, CAPM.
- **Uses:** The CAPM is a mathematical method for estimating the profitability of any financial asset. The return forecast is calculated according to the risk that the asset entails.
- **Why is it successful?** The CAPM is one of the most popular risk assessment methods for financial assets. However, its effectiveness has been criticised by economists such as Richard Roll (American economist, born in 1939).
- **Key words:**
  - Capital market: A meeting place between supply and demand for capital. Supply corresponds to savings (the surplus of available capital) made available to those wishing to borrow. Those who borrow constitute the demand (the need for financing). Balance in this market is crucial.
  - Financial asset: An asset is a security or a contract that gives the holder the opportunity to obtain a gain in return for a given risk. For example: I buy shares (a financial asset), in the hope that in time their value will increase and I can sell them to earn a profit. However, if the share value decreases, I will make a loss on my purchase.
  - Interest rate: The interest rate represents the cost of money. It therefore allows me to calculate the costs involved in borrowing or investing money. The interest

rate can also be defined as the remuneration obtained in the case of investments.

- ○ <u>Portfolio:</u> All the transferable securities (in particular stocks and bonds) held by a person, a company, a bank, etc.

- ○ <u>Returns:</u> The profitability of an amount invested. If I invest my money with an interest rate of 7% and a friend invests the same amount with a 4% interest rate, I can say that my return on capital invested is better than his.

- ○ <u>Stock exchange:</u> A public or private institution that allows exchanges of assets and transactions of securities (such as shares) to take place. In other words, it is a financing and investment market where the price is set according to supply and demand.

INTRODUCTION

In the 1950s, the financial markets developed and became the ideal intermediary for balancing the capacities and funding requirements of various economic agents. Their aim was to ensure the financing of the economy through a range of means (savings, security purchases, asset purchases, etc.). Two closely related variables are involved in the investment of a financial asset: returns and risk.

In order to better define these two variables, studies were carried out by various economists:

- Frank Knight (American economist, 1885-1972) defined the concepts of 'uncertainty' and 'risk' in 1921.

- The work of Harry Markowitz (American economist, born in 1927) marked the beginning of the modern theory of diversification in 1950, known as modern portfolio theory since 1952. This theory puts forward a financial reflection on the use of diversification to optimise a portfolio. This is the most similar version to the current CAPM.
- Finally, in the 1960s and early 1970s, the American economists William Sharpe (born in 1934), John Lintner (1916-1983) and Fischer Black (1938-1995), and the Norwegian economist Jan Mossin (1936-1987), developed earlier financial models, giving rise to the CAPM.

DEFINITION OF THE MODEL

The CAPM is used both on the financial markets and to solve financial problems in business. The calculation model is based on the measurement of systematic risk, expected profitability and interest rates. In other words, the CAPM enables the return on an asset, relative to its risk, to be estimated.

THEORY

This section provides information on the method of evaluation of financial assets from a purely theoretical point of view in order to allow all the nuances of the CAPM to be grasped.

CONTEXT

This model was developed at a time when all the financial markets were improving and becoming standardised. It was created because investors wanted to be more aware of the risks of a financial investment.

Markowitz's contribution

The CAPM extends Markowitz's modern portfolio theory, both in its assumptions and in its conclusions. Markowitz emphasised the benefits of portfolio diversification for investors who want to obtain the best risk-return ratio.

Markowitz includes five assumptions in his model:

1. financial markets are efficient, meaning that the price and returns of financial assets always accurately present all of the information available on these assets;
2. investors are risk-averse and therefore take no additional risks without the guarantee of any additional return;
3. the markets are balanced;
4. there is no arbitrage opportunity on balanced markets, since the supply of assets would perfectly match the

demand for these assets and the price would then be naturally balanced;

5. and finally, the investor makes rational choices.

DEFINITIONS

- <u>Arbitrage opportunity</u>: The possibility for an investor to change their asset portfolio according to their anticipations. Specifically, it is an operation (buying or selling) which is reversed for two different markets, two products or two deadlines. The opportunity involves taking advantage of trading anomalies.
- <u>Asset correlation</u>: The relationship between two financial assets going in the same direction (positive correlation) or in the opposite direction (negative correlation).

Markowitz's contributions are twofold. On the one hand, he raises the fact that the advantages of the diversification of asset portfolios are not based on the lack of correlation between returns, but rather on their imperfect or partial correlation. On the other hand, he demonstrates that the risk reduction linked to diversification is limited by the degree of correlation between assets. Consequently, Markowitz shows that diversification reduces risk without affecting profitability.

The capital asset pricing model, meanwhile, extends the scope because it considers all economic agents.

THE MAIN AIM OF THE CAPM

As previously stated, the aim of the CAPM is to give the investor as much information as possible about the risks and potential profitability of the financial asset in which they want to invest. The savvy investor opts for either an efficient risky portfolio, or a balance between risky and non-risky assets. The CAPM allows the equilibrium price of assets to be established.

ASSUMPTIONS OF THE MODEL

DEFINITIONS

- Standard deviation: The most commonly used measure of dispersion to outline a central trend. It therefore measures the variability in relation to the mean.
- Expectancy: Representation of the average gain or loss that a person is likely to receive as part of a random experiment.

- All investors are considered to be 'investors' according to Markowitz's definition: they consider each asset only in terms of risk/profitability. The market is without 'friction', meaning that there are no transaction costs, no commission, etc.
- Capital gains and dividends are not taxed.
- The market is balanced, and an investor can buy or sell

any asset as long as it has no impact on the share price; information is transparent.

- Investors do not like risk-free investments. This is why they choose a higher or lower level of risk depending the compensation they could obtain from it (risk premium).
- Investors have the same time horizon, which allows the analyses to be somewhat standardised.
- Investors anticipate the future performance of the securities in the same way.
- Investments are infinitely divisible: it is possible to buy or sell fractions of shares or portfolios.
- Investors control risk through diversification.
- Investors may lend or borrow any sum of money at a risk-free rate.
- The profitability of an asset is estimated using the expected gain at a given horizon, and its risk is estimated using the standard deviation of its past variations. For example, a relatively risky share will show fluctuating prices and therefore a higher standard deviation.

Assume that there is homogeneity in expectancies, standard deviations and variations as well as the correlations between different financial assets.

Furthermore, each portfolio is composed of the same type of asset. Only the proportion – the percentage of risk (low or high) – of risky and non-risky assets is different.

COMPONENTS OF THE MODEL

The CAPM is based on the fact that the different assets and asset portfolios are analysed in terms of their risk-return ratio, and the challenge facing each investor is to aim for a portfolio with maximum utility. There are three essential components to put together an efficient portfolio:

- the capital market line, which detects the different risk-return combinations;
- the market premium, which defines the cost of risk;
- the beta coefficient, which measures the risk of an asset in relation to the market risk.

The capital market line (CML)

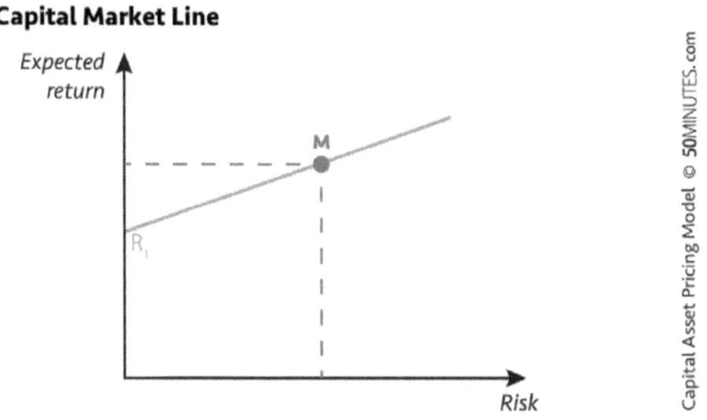

The capital market line shows the risk-return combinations of financial assets. R_f is the level of profitability for a risk-free asset (for example, government bonds), while M refers to the overall combination observed on the market, also called the market portfolio. The choice of the combination will depend on the investor profile and their risk aversion.

Capital market line formula

$$E(R_i) = R_f + \left(\frac{E(R_M) - R_f}{\sigma_M} \right) \sigma$$

i : asset

M : market

σ : risk

$(E(R_M) - R_f)$: risk premium

$E(R_i)$: expected profitability of the asset

R_f : profitability of the asset or risk-free interest rate

Market premium and the CAPM

The investor needs a market premium that covers the risk taken. The greater the risk, the higher the premium and the steeper the CLM slope.

The beta risk indicator

The CAPM does not measure the level of risk, but rather the relative risk of the asset or portfolio in relation to the market, called ß (beta). In other words, beta is the relationship between changes in the price of a financial asset (this is known as 'volatility') and changes in prices on the market in general. This is the sensitivity or elasticity of the price of an asset, relative to the stock index representing the market. The closer the value of beta is to 1, the less volatile the asset is considered to be.

The risk premium for a financial asset is therefore equal to its beta coefficient multiplied by the overall market risk.

The CAPM is equal to the risk premium of an asset *i* or a portfolio and the market risk premium multiplied by the beta value of the asset under consideration.

Capital asset pricing model formula

$$E(R_i) = R_f + \beta_i \, [\, E(R_M) - R_f \,]$$

i : asset

$E(R_i)$: expected profitability of the asset

R_f : profitability of the asset or risk-free interest rate

β_i : measure of the systematic risk of the asset (non-diversifiable risk of the asset)

$E(R_M)$: expected profitability of the market

The expected return for the asset *i* (*E(R_i)*) can be calculated as long as the risk-free rate, the beta of the asset and the market premium are known. Conversely, if the return is known, the risk can also be calculated.

ADVANTAGES

DID YOU KNOW?

The discount rate is the rate that allows a future value to be turned into a current value, taking into account that the longer the duration between the present and the future, the more the current value decreases.

Discount rate formula

$$ANV = F_0 + \frac{F_1}{(1 + t_\%)} + \frac{F_2}{(1 + t_\%)^2} + \frac{F_3}{(1 + t_\%)^3} + \dots + \frac{F_n}{(1 + t_\%)^n}$$

ANV : actual net value

F : future fluctuations

t : discount rate

The CAPM offers several advantages:

- it allows the different returns for the assets in question to be calculated;
- it facilitates economic and financial decision-making by calculating risk;
- the model is simpler to use than arbitrage pricing theory, although it is less accurate from an econometric point of view;
- there are two useful applications for the model:
  - measuring the performance of fund managers;
  - calculating the appropriate discount rate to assess the future income of a company.

CONCLUSION

It is therefore understandable that, in general, a rational investor will opt for a diversified portfolio of financial assets (risky and non-risky assets) in order to ensure maximum efficiency and limited risk.

Although it is difficult to assess its effectiveness, the CAPM remains a performance measurement tool that allows users to compare the work of management and market realities, and also indicates the appropriate discount rate to calculate the future revenue of a business.

LIMITATIONS AND EXTENSIONS

LIMITATIONS AND CRITICISMS

The limitations of the CAPM are numerous and the criticisms are mostly related to the prior assumptions made.

- **The instability of beta.** As a reminder, beta is the relative risk of an asset or portfolio in comparison with the rest of the market. This instability stems from the fact that the risk of an asset is variable and therefore subject to change at any time. For example, imagine that I buy a financial asset at time t and I calculate the risk x that I am taking with this investment. At this point, there is no guarantee that at time $t + 1$, the risk x of that asset will not have changed due to external factors (such as a crisis). To overcome this flaw, the manager generally considers all the betas in order to partly reduce the individual risk.
- **The limit of portfolio diversification.** It is impossible to fully diversify a portfolio: investors should buy a number of diversified financial assets before aiming for partial correlation (in the event that diversification reduces risk). In addition, a portfolio with a reduced correlation can end up correlating because of the changing economic, social and political context.
- **The difficulty of practical application** in a forecasting context.
- **The unrealistic assumptions.** It is almost impossible to have a precise idea of the risk-free rates in which to invest; there is no uniform taxation between financial assets, whereas transaction costs are very real, etc.

- **The dependence of studies of the CAPM on market portfolio choices.** This dependence was elaborated by the economist Richard Roll.

WEAKNESSES AND CRITICISMS

On a wider scale, critics challenge the relative efficiency of the CAPM.

As such, Roll questions whether it is possible to test the effectiveness of the model: according to him, in order to verify it, we would need to be able to measure the efficiency of the market portfolio, which he considers to be impossible. He argues that, since the portfolio includes not only all the shares but also bonds, real estate and precious metals, among other things, it cannot be measured precisely and integrated effectively into the CAPM.

RELATED MODELS AND EXTENSIONS

While the CAPM is based solely on the evaluation of the beta, a tool for measuring variable risk, other models offer alternative methods which also allow the financial risk to be determined.

Arbitrage pricing theory (APT)

Given the volatility of the betas observed in the CAPM, in 1976 Stephen Alan Ross (American economist, born in 1944) presented an alternative model based on the theory of arbitrage.

According to him, there are several economic factors that influence profitability:

- on the one hand, general factors that simultaneously affect the profitability of several assets;
- on the other hand, factors specific to an asset that only influence the profitability of that asset.

The theory of arbitrage further claims that the factors specific to different assets are independent of the general factors and are also independent from each other.

The principle of arbitrage occurs when two assets, with the same sensitivities to different factors, do not have the same expected return. If there is no arbitrage opportunity, meaning they have the same expected return, the market risk of the asset must be calculated using the betas relating to the non-specific market factors that affect all investments.

The APT is applied more generally than the CAPM. However, its main weakness lies in the origin and choice of factors influencing the assets.

Multifactor model

The multifactor model attempts to overcome the shortcoming of the APT, namely the identification of specific economic factors that may influence the risk. Since the market risk affects most (if not all) investments, it comes from macroeconomic factors. The model thus defines market risk as the risk of exposure of any asset to macroeconomic factors. For this model, the basis for calculating risk is the beta of the asset, relative to macroeconomic factors.

Fama-French three-factor model or representative variable model

This model was developed in the early 1990s by American economists Eugene Francis Fama and Kenneth Ronald French and draws inspiration from the multifactorial model, which states that return is influenced by more than one factor. The Fama-French model highlights the existence of two factors that influence the return:

- **The size of the company.** Fama and French measure the size of a company using market capitalisation (MC). They note in particular that assets from small MC companies, considered riskier and with a higher cost of capital, have a high average return compared to larger MC companies. As a result, securities from small MC companies have surplus return compared to risk-free assets, which is higher than that predicted by the CAPM.
- Like market capitalisation, **the shares with a higher book-to-market ratio**, relatively underestimated by the market, are riskier and have a higher cost of capital. However, it is often these shares that have the highest returns.

By comparing the MC and the book-to market ratio, Fama and French find that the book-to market ratio is statistically more relevant than the MC and is a major factor that has a strong influence on assets. Moreover, in the long term, they noticed that the relationship between the book-to market ratio and the return is much stronger and more stable than the relationship between the MV and returns.

In conclusion, profitable investments are made in companies with low market capitalisation and a high book value, which could not be considered in the CAPM model.

PRACTICAL APPLICATION

This section provides information on the steps to follow and the questions to ask when implementing the CAPM. It also provides useful recommendations in order to avoid making errors.

ADVICE AND BEST PRACTICES

Defining the risk of an investment

The first step is to define the risk of an investment. This risk can be measured using the variance of the actual profitability, relative to the anticipated income. The risk level of the asset can then be observed: no risk, low risk or high risk.

Types of investment

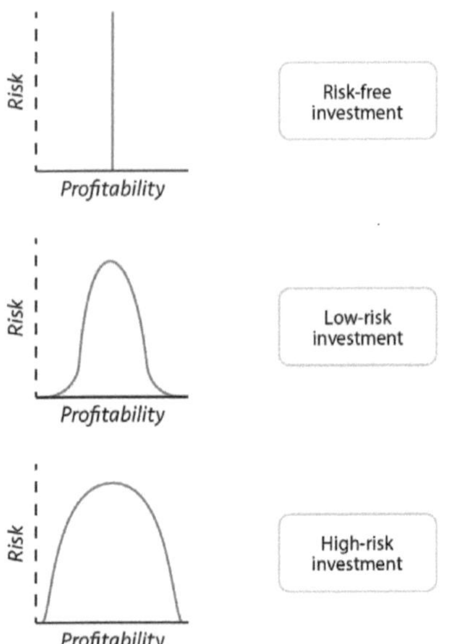

Distinguishing between paid and non-paid risks

Once the level of risk has been determined, it is necessary to differentiate between paid and non-paid risks. Each particular asset has two types of risk: the risk specific to an investment, called the 'business risk' or 'inherent risk', and the general risk of all investments, called the 'market risk'.

- **The specific risk** can be controlled in a diversified portfolio if the specific risky investment is only a small part of the portfolio and may, for example, be counterbalanced by a less risky specific asset. We then talk about 'medium risk', which refers to the different specific risk investments from a single portfolio.

- **The market risk,** which affects all investments, cannot be controlled because it generally covers all of the financial assets on the market. There are two factors behind this risk: general developments in the economic world – from taxation to pricing policy – and how investors feel about these potential developments.

The savvy investor, having usually ensured that they have a diversified portfolio, will not be compensated for the risks related to market changes.

Measuring the market risk

To calculate this risk, the investor may use different methods, including the CAPM, the APT, the multi-factor model and the French-Fama model outlined above. Depending on the assumptions made, the market risk is perceived and calculated differently.

The CAPM is based on the fact that individual assets and portfolios are judged according to the risk-return ratio and that the goal of every investor is to seek the most efficient portfolio. This can be achieved in three steps.

1. The investor must determine the 'efficient frontier', meaning the collection of portfolios that minimise the risk for a given average return. This collection of portfolios is called the efficient set, and is represented by the area inside the umbrella shape. Below, we see that the point

x is not rational, as for the same level of risk, there is a combination of higher return, *e*.

Efficient frontier of portfolios

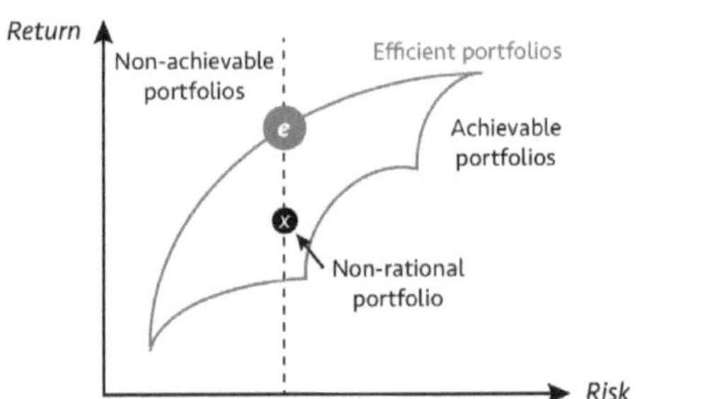

The sum of the amounts invested should equal 1. The weaker the correlation coefficient, the more the risk is reduced: the indifference curve then moves to the left.

Indifference curve

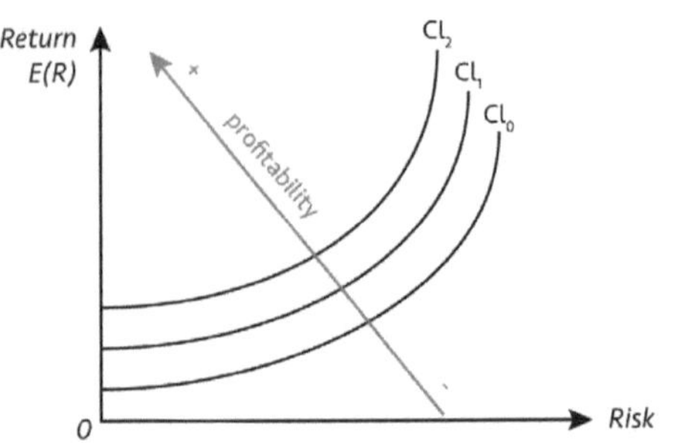

The indifference curve is the set of combinations of two goods or two factors which provide the consumer or investor with the same level of satisfaction. The Y-axis, *E(R)*, corresponds to the expected return, while the X-axis corresponds to the risk level. As each curve gives the investor the same satisfaction, for a different risk-return combination and whatever the specific indifference curve, they will choose the portfolio with the highest return for a given risk.

2. Depending on their attitude to risk (indifference curve), the investor chooses 'their' optimal portfolio. This corresponds to the point of tangency between the indifference curve and the efficient frontier. If they consider a risk-free asset, the investor will be able to invest part of their assets in one of the riskier portfolios on the efficient frontier of risky assets, and another part in a risk-free asset.

3. To measure this risk mathematically, the investor must use the formula set out in the theoretical definition of the concept:

Capital asset pricing model formula

$$E(R_i) = R_f + \beta_i \, [\, E(R_M) - R_f \,]$$

4. Moreover, it is common knowledge that the evaluations of financial assets are carried out by computers nowadays.

RECOMMENDATIONS

Necessary assumptions and variants of the model

When applying the CAPM, it is important to be aware that the model is not always realistic: given the current situation, the assumptions made by the model are rarely valid. The calculation of the risk-return ratio should therefore be extended to broader assumptions and variants. Below are some examples of the contradictions observed:

- The model only considers the securities traded on the stock exchange in the market portfolio. A market portfolio should be defined by all the existing investment opportunities in the economy, and therefore is much broader.
- The CAPM makes assumptions that are difficult to apply in the current context. The theoretical model must therefore be extended to the reality of our environment, which often makes it less relevant and more complex.
- Zero beta or no risk. It is usually impossible to borrow at a risk-free rate. You cannot really assume that a risk-free asset exists. The CAPM must be adapted to suit this reality.
- The CAPM also assumes that there is no tax, no transaction costs, etc. This assumption should be reconsidered, as investors are subject to tax (including dividends and capital gains on sale) and transaction costs. If all of these additional costs are taken into account, investors will tend to limit the size of their portfolios by buying fewer shares.

There are many extensions of the assumptions and variants on the model. In particular, in chapter 3 of his book Quantitative Financial Economics: Stocks, Bonds and Foreign Exchange, Keith Cuthbertson presents and develops the nuances of the CAPM and their mathematical applications.

Finally, it is recommended that the investor or investing company considers the 'diversification' factor, an essential parameter in measuring risk, in order to reduce the risk. Moreover, caution should be exercised, as there is no such thing as risk-free return! Generally, portfolio diversification is one of the best ways to protect investors and limit risk.

Stocks

The increase in the number of assets in the portfolio is associated with decreased risk, although this is not a linear development. The effects of diversification are significant at first, but after a certain point they diminish while costs related to the number of shares (transactions, fixed costs, etc.) grow. Furthermore, maximum diversification reduces the variability of returns on stocks. For example, if the variability is reduced by 70%, the remaining 30% constitutes the 'systematic' risk because it is impossible to completely eliminate risk through diversification (see market risk).

ACTIVE AND PASSIVE MANAGEMENT

- Active management generally offers a higher risk than the market risk for a higher expected return.
- Passive management guarantees a risk equivalent

Diversification can be done at different levels:

- in different zones (Europe, USA, Japan, emerging countries, etc.)
- on the level of sectors of activity
- according to the company size
- by management style (active, passive, etc.)

In addition to shares, we can take other examples such as bonds, cash and gold, without taking into account other assets such as investment funds, artworks, etc.

- **Bonds** generally offer lower returns than shares, but the risk is limited.
- **Cash or savings** offer mostly lower returns than shares – with exceptions such as Fortis shares, which lost about 95% of their value in 2008 –, but with the same order of magnitude as bonds.
- **Gold** is characterised by a high risk for a lower average return than other assets.

CASE STUDY

Context

In the context of wealth management, a manager defines the objective of the client in order to best meet it. The expert analyses the whole situation of the investor – family, work, take and property. This analysis allows them to specify more specific needs.

What is the most efficient portfolio for this investor-client according to the CAPM model?

The problem lies in the assessment and determination of an efficient portfolio depending on the type of investor the wealth manager is dealing with.

Firstly, the manager must determine several market parameters:

- **The choice of the reference market portfolio.** There are several stock indexes which bring together a representative set of assets on the markets. These include the CAC 40, which features the 40 largest market capitalisations in France, and the S&P 500 in America.
- **The choice of risk-free asset.** We can consider government bonds or life insurance products to be assets with a limited risk. Although the risk is limited – and therefore never completely zero – the return is uncertain and volatile.
- **The choice of customer portfolio.** The CAPM assumes that all the financial assets on the market are correctly assessed: they each have a particular risk and expected return. The manager chooses with the investor, who is aware of the inevitable relationship between the return on assets and the risks, the portfolio that most closely matches the client's expectations. The choice of portfolio content for the client will therefore be directly related to their exposure to the market portfolio. This coefficient of exposure (beta) can easily be obtained through financial information relayed by the stock index. Once the beta is determined, it is useful to establish a strategy to meet the investor's requirements.
- **Model variants: beta, volatility and portfolio performance.** Calculating the parameters of the CAPM can be done in different ways:
  - Using previous historical data based on episodic effects. However, this requires caution: as changes in

historical data are generally tied to specific periods (for example, periods of crisis), they do not provide complete objectivity.

◦ Through financial data which is already available and in use across various platforms. Again, it is important to be careful, as some analyses may be about the subjective and biased.

◦ Finally, through corporate reports and economic forecasts.

In general, the manager seeks the most complete – and therefore most reliable – information in order to avoid adding further risk to the investor's portfolio. Once the variants of the model have been specified, the CAPM determines the best possible distribution of the investor's financial resources, while respecting their wishes in terms of returns, risk and types of assets.

Portfolio simulation

Imagine a relatively diversified portfolio with assets in different sectors, issued by companies of varying importance, investing in different geographic markets.

This portfolio comprises 15 German government bonds, 20 shares in Belfius, 8 shares in a Cambodian agricultural cooperative and 10 other shares in American real estate.

Knowing the level of correlation is important because it allows us to work out whether the portfolio is very risky (coefficient close to 1; positive correlation) or not (coefficient close to 0; negative correlation). Furthermore, the performance coefficient gives information on the level of risk control and therefore the relative security of the assets. This performance is calculated using the ratio of economist William Sharpe so that any negative result is removed from the portfolio.

Sharpe ratio

$$\text{Sharpe ratio} = \frac{\text{profit} - \text{risk-free rate}}{\text{volatility}}$$

The performance analysis can include two dimensions:

- a graphical dimension
- a mathematical dimension, expressed by portfolio value and the value of the assets that make up the portfolio.

In the case of our portfolio, we can see that the diversification adopted is good but can be improved, in particular by choosing less correlated assets.

Conclusion

The CAPM enables a simple analysis of market movements and the exposure to risk of given assets. However, without the extensions of the model, it is of little – or no – use and is inefficient. The Sharpe ratio, for example, is an important tool to measure the performance of the assets in a complex environment like that of today.

SUMMARY

- The CAPM is a mathematical method which allows the expected return of any financial asset to be calculated.
- The model appeared in the 1950s, at a time when the financial markets were developing and becoming standardised, as investors wanted more information and safeguards to ensure the profitability of their financial assets.
- Theorists:
    - in 1921, Frank Knight defined the concepts of uncertainty and risk;
    - in 1950, the work of Harry Markowitz marked the beginning of the modern theory of diversification and portfolios;
    - finally, from 1964 onwards, economists such as William Sharpe, John Lintner, Jan Mossin and Fischer Black developed existing financial models, which led to the creation of the CAPM.
- When applying the model, it is essential to:
    - determine the efficient frontier of portfolios;
    - determine the optimal portfolio, by diversifying the asset portfolio to minimise the systematic risk while maintaining a certain level of profitability.
    - measure the risk and profitability of the portfolio.
- The model is only useful if there is no missing information and no transaction costs. The optimal diversified portfolio is therefore the same for all investors.
- The main limitations of this model are the inapplicability of the assumptions made and the instability of the beta

value.

- Three models are extensions to the CAPM: the APT (arbitrage pricing theory), the multi-factor model and the Fama-French three-factor model.

We want to hear from you!
Leave a comment on your online library
and share your favourite books on social media!

FURTHER READING

BIBLIOGRAPHY

- Baudot, J.-Y. (No date) Le MÉDAF. *JYBaudot.fr*. [Online]. [Accessed 26 June 2014]. Available from: <http://www.jybaudot.fr/Bourse/medaf.html>
- Broquet, C., Cobbaut, R., Gillet, R. and van den Berg, A. (2004) *Gestion de portefeuille*. Brussels: De Boeck.
- Damodaran, A. (2006) *Finance d'entreprise. Théorie et pratique*. Brussels: De Boeck.
- Desquilbet, J.-B. (No date) Le MÉDAF. Modèle d'évaluation des actifs financiers. *Université d'Artois*. [Online]. [Accessed 26 June 2014]. Available from: <http://jb.desquilbet.pagesperso-orange.fr/docs/A_M2thfi_2_MEDAF.pdf>
- Gaga, O. and Tarib, A. (No date) Le Modèle d'Équilibre des Actifs Financiers. Cas d'ITISSALAT AL-MAGHRIB. *Scribd*. [Online]. [Accessed 26 June 2014]. Available from: <http://fr.scribd.com/doc/24407264/Modele-d-equilibre-des-actifs-financiers-MEDAF-CAPM>
- Limaiem, I. (2009) Les facteurs du modèle Fama et French : cas du marché des actions canadiennes. *Université du Québec à Montréal*. [Online]. [Accessed 8 July 2014]. Available from: <http://www.archipel.uqam.ca/2202/1/M10858.pdf>
- Moisson, J.-C. (No date) *Méthodes et principes de gestion de portefeuille benchmarkée*. [Online]. [Accessed 26 June 2014]. Available from: <http://www.bm.com.tn/ckeditor/files/gestion_de_portefeuille_bench.pdf>
- Ngoma, F. (2009) Évaluation des actifs financiers par le

MÉDAF. Validation empirique de la relation risque-rendement par les modèles économétriques. *Mémoire Online.* [Online]. [Accessed 26 June 2014]. Available from: <http://www.memoireonline.com/07/10/3749/ Evaluation-des-actifs-financiers-par-le-MEDAF- validation-empirique-de-la-relation-risque-rendement-. html>

- Statistics Canada (No date) *Variance and standard deviation.* [Online]. [Accessed 26 June 2014]. Available from: <http://www.statcan.gc.ca/edu/power-pouvoir/ ch12/5214891-eng.htm>

ADDITIONAL SOURCES

- Back, K.E. (2010) *Asset Pricing and Portfolio Choice Theory (Financial Management Association Survey and Synthesis).* New York: Oxford University Press USA.
- Capinski, M.J. and Kopp, E. (2014) *Portfolio Theory and Risk Management (Mastering Mathematical Finance).* Cambridge: Cambridge University Press.
- Cuthbertson, K. and Nitzsche, D. (2004) *Quantitative Financial Economics: Stocks, Bonds and Foreign Exchange.* [2nd edition]. West Sussex: John Wiley & Sons.
- Levy, H. (2011) *The Capital Asset Pricing Model in the 21st Century: Analytical, Empirical, and Behavioral Perspectives.* New York: Cambridge University Press.